Lorde

By
Adrianna Morganelli

Crabtree Publishing Company
www.crabtreebooks.com

Crabtree Publishing Company

www.crabtreebooks.com

Author: Adrianna Morganelli
Publishing plan research and development: Reagan Miller
Photo research: Tammy McGarr
Editor: Kathy Middleton
Proofreader and Indexer: Wendy Scavuzzo
Designer: Ken Wright
Production coordinator and prepress technician: Ken Wright
Print coordinator: Margaret Amy Salter

Photographs:
Creative Commons: Liliane Callegari: p. 15;
Corbis: © Paul R. Giunta: p. 6; © Daniel DeSlover/ZUMA Press/Corbis: p. 7; © Fern/Splash News/Corbis: p. 10; © Splash News: p. 27;
Everett Collection: ©Lionsgate: p. 23
Getty Images: Amanda Edwards: front cover, p. 4; Kevin Mazur/AMA2014 / contributor: p. 5; Lester Cohen / contributor: p. 8, 12; Hannah Peters / staff: p. 9; Mark Davis / staff: p. 13; Fiona Goodall / stringer: p. 14; Roger Kisby / contributor: p. 16; Dimitrios Kambouris / staff: p. 18; Theo Wargo / staff: p. 19; Chelsea Lauren / contributor: p. 21; Axelle/Bauer-Griffin / contributor: p. 22; Christopher Polk / staff: p. 24; Frazer Harrison / staff: 28; Brendon Thorne / stringer: p. 25
Keystone: © wenn.com: title page; ZUMAPRESS.com: pp. 17, 26 (top);
Photoshot: © Face to Face p. 20; p. 26 (bottom)
Wikimedia Commons: Mike Reardon: p. 11;

Library and Archives Canada Cataloguing in Publication

Morganelli, Adrianna, 1979- , author
Lorde / Adrianna Morganelli.

(Superstars!)
Includes index.
Issued in print and electronic formats.
ISBN 978-0-7787-8080-9 (bound).--ISBN 978-0-7787-8084-7 (pbk.).--ISBN 978-1-4271-9986-7 (pdf).--ISBN 978-1-4271-9982-9 (html)

1. Lorde, 1996- --Juvenile literature. 2. Singers--New Zealand--Biography--Juvenile literature. I. Title. II. Series: Superstars! (St. Catharines, Ont.)

ML3930.L67M67 2015 j782.42164092 C2014-907837-4
C2014-907838-2

Library of Congress Cataloging-in-Publication Data

Morganelli, Adrianna, 1979- author.
Lorde / Adrianna Morganelli.
pages ; cm. -- (Superstars!)
Includes an index.
ISBN 978-0-7787-8080-9 (reinforced library binding : alk. paper) -- ISBN 978-0-7787-8084-7 (pbk. : alk. paper) -- ISBN 978-1-4271-9986-7 (electronic pdf : alk. paper) -- ISBN 978-1-4271-9982-9 (electronic html : alk. paper)
1. Lorde, 1996---Juvenile literature. 2. Singers--New Zealand--Biography--Juvenile literature. I. Title.

ML3930.L67M67 2015
782.42164092--dc23
[B]

2014046863

Crabtree Publishing Company

Printed in Canada/042015/BF20150203

www.crabtreebooks.com 1-800-387-7650

Published in Canada
Crabtree Publishing
616 Welland Ave.
St. Catharines, ON
L2M 5V6

Published in the United States
Crabtree Publishing
PMB 59051
350 Fifth Avenue, 59th Floor
New York, New York 10118

Published in the United Kingdom
Crabtree Publishing
Maritime House
Basin Road North, Hove
BN41 1WR

Published in Australia
Crabtree Publishing
3 Charles Street
Coburg North
VIC 3058

CONTENTS

Words that are defined in the glossary are in bold type the first time they appear in the text.

Heroine of the Story

Lorde is a singer and songwriter from New Zealand who created a buzz when she arrived on the pop music scene in 2013. Her deep voice and honest lyrics about what it's truly like to be a teenager today have won her countless fans and praise from critics who call her a musical phenomenon. Lorde's debut album, *Pure Heroine,* has sold more than two million copies worldwide and earned the young singer two Grammy awards—all by the age of just 17.

In 2013, *TIME* magazine listed Lorde as one of the most influential teens in the world.

Serious Pop

Lorde's music is a combination of pop, rock, **indietronica**, and dream pop. Dream pop is a type of music that focuses on sound, and is made up of breathy vocals and guitar effects. Like most pop songs, her lyrics focus on themes that teens can identify with, such as romance, social anxiety, parties, and boredom.

But Lorde's songwriting goes deeper. The lyrics in her hit singles "Royals," "Team," and "Tennis Court," criticize what most other pop stars **glorify**, such as living lavish lifestyles and only being concerned about what other people think of you. Lorde has been hailed as a unique voice speaking up for her generation as well as for teenagers—an age group whose opinions are often dismissed.

She Said It

"For a long time pop has been this laughable, shameful thing. But it's actually gratifying and fun and can unite populations, which I think is incredibly powerful. So hopefully I am showing that pop can be taken seriously."
—Interview in *The Telegraph*, January 2014

From Ella to Lorde

Like most musicians, Lorde uses a different professional, or stage, name. Her real name is Ella Marija Lani Yelich-O'Connor. As a child, Ella was fascinated by the extravagant lives of royalty and the wealthy **aristocracy**. It inspired her to choose the word "lord" when trying to come up with a stage name. Lord is a term used to address people born into noble families who pass down their titles from father to son. Lords are traditionally men, so Ella added an "e" on the end to make it feminine.

Name That Style

Lorde's sense of fashion is an important part of her stage presentation. Topped with a thick mane of curly hair, the singer is often seen in videos and photographs wearing her signature dark-purple lipstick and black eyeliner. Her style has been described at times as goth, punk, grunge, or architectural. In reality, it includes a little bit of all these styles. Lorde has said that she just likes to dress up in beautiful clothes that make her feel powerful and strong.

Still a teen, Lorde has already developed her own sense of style. Her style icons include singers David Bowie and Grace Jones.

She Said It

"The way I dress and carry myself, a lot of people find it strange or intimidating. I think my whole career can be boiled down to the one word I always say in meetings: strength."
—*Rolling Stone* magazine, January 2014

On Each Other's Team

Ella Yelich-O'Connor was born on November 7, 1996, in the beach area of Takapuna, in New Zealand. She was raised in Devonport, Auckland, with her two sisters Jerry and India, and her brother Angelo.

Ella's parents' roots are Irish and Croatian.

Family Influence

Ella is the second-oldest child of Vic O'Connor, a **civil engineer**, and Sonja Yelich, who is an award-winning poet. Sonja encouraged all her children to read a variety of books and bought them children's and adults' books. Ella recalls that there weren't any books that she wasn't allowed to read. Despite living in New Zealand, she grew up listening to American music artists, including the **soul** music of Otis Redding and Etta James. Her parents played their favorite records by Neil Young, Fleetwood Mac, and Cat Stevens.

Love and Support

Ella's parents believed in creating a very positive atmosphere at home. All the children were encouraged to express their opinions and take advantage of opportunities. Ella clearly benefited. At six, she attended a school for gifted learning for several weeks. However, her mother ultimately decided to take her out of it. She was afraid Ella might lose her connection to the rest of the world if she was in a school that set her apart. It also certainly helped that Ella loved school. She admits to being a perfectionist, and she says she always took her schoolwork very seriously.

"Team" was named Single of the Year at the New Zealand Music Awards in 2014. Ella brought her brother and sister with her onstage to accept the award.

She Said It

"We're one of the louder, more insane families. We're all super creative and impulsive. It's been a good environment to learn how to speak your mind, you know? And be feisty. And unapologetic. But weirdly, I'm the quietest member of my family. It took me a while to be able to find a voice in terms of being able to talk to people."

—Interview on tvnz.co.nz, May 15, 2014

Ella loves to shop at thrift stores, which are called opportunity shops, or op shops, in New Zealand.

Developing Her Interests

When Ella was five, she went with a friend to a drama group. She soon discovered that she enjoyed acting and singing, and continued to attend the classes herself for eight years. As a young teen, she often went to the theater to see movies. Her favorites are horror movies and thrillers. She also went on regular outings with her mother to art museums and bookstores. Interested in clothing, even as a kid, she shopped at thrift stores. She then cut the clothes up and put different styles together. Her unusual style and taste in books made her stand out—sometimes to the point of being teased.

Quiz Kid

Ella entered short story and speech competitions, and came in second with her school team at the 2009 Kids Literature Quiz held in South Africa.

Battle at Belmont

By the age of 12, music was taking center stage in Ella's life. She formed a duo with her friend Louis McDonald, and they entered the annual talent competition at her school, Belmont Intermediate. With Louis playing the guitar, Ella sang two cover songs, "Warwick Avenue" by Duffy and "Mama Do" by Pixie Lotts. Their flawless performance won the competition. Louis's father was so impressed with their performance that he sent a video of it to the record label Universal Music Group (UMG).

During the same year, Ella entered the school's Battle of the Bands competition with some schoolmates. They formed a band called Extreme, in which she was the lead singer. They performed two songs—"Man On The Silver Mountain" by Rainbow and "Edie (Ciao Baby)" by The Cult. Extreme placed third in the competition.

Ella and Louis

Sign on the Line

By this time, Scott Maclachlan, an **artists and repertoire (A&R) manager** at Universal Music Group, had watched the video Louis's father had sent in. Scott could tell that Ella was destined to be a star. But Ella's mother was very unhappy when she found out that the tape had been sent in without her knowledge. Sonja felt that 12 was too young to be thrown into the music business. But Ella saw it as an opportunity and her parents allowed her to pursue it. Maclachlan became her manager, and UMG signed Ella to their label with the intention of developing her voice. She was given singing lessons twice a week with a voice coach, and she learned how to use her voice effectively. Maclachlan wanted her to put out an album of soul cover songs, but Ella refused. She didn't want to sing other people's songs. She wanted to write her own.

Lorde poses with two executives from Universal Music Group in January 2014.

Collaboration

Her manager tried putting Ella together with a number of different songwriters and **producers**, but she found it an uncomfortable way to write. Then, in December 2011, Maclachlan paired Ella with Joel Little, a songwriter and record producer who began his career as a guitarist and lead singer for the New Zealand pop punk band Goodnight Nurse. The two clicked creatively! Since Ella was still in school, they met on weekends and during school holidays to write music. Little was impressed by Ella's voice and songwriting ability, and he taught her about song structure.

Lorde's songwriting partner, Joel Little

She Said It

"It wasn't until I had vocal lessons, when I was thirteen or fourteen, that singing really became kind of a tool, and something I could use to get across what I was feeling. Before then, the things that I had taught myself to do with my throat were instinctive, and stuff that I was mimicking from things that I had heard. I had quite a nasal, twangy voice."

–Interview in *Vogue*, February 20, 2014

Different Kind of Buzz

The pairing of Ella and Joel Little was so harmonious that in just three weeks, they completed *The Love Club* **EP**. At his production studio in Auckland, Joel composed the melodies for the songs on the EP, and the two of them wrote the lyrics together. The five songs were "Royals," "Bravado," "Biting Down," "Million Dollar Bills," and "The Love Club."

Lorde and Joel accept the Song of the Year award for "Royals" at the Grammys.

She Said It

"Ella's a better writer than I'll ever be. A couple of years ago, I wrote a thesis for my master's, and I asked Ella to proofread it – 40,000 words. She did an incredible job. And she was 14." —Sonja Yelich, in *Rolling Stone* magazine, October 28, 2013

The Love Club EP

Ella and her manager decided to release *The Love Club EP* as a free download on Facebook, Twitter, Tumblr, and SoundCloud, which is a social sound platform that allows users to upload, record, and **promote** their original music. They knew young listeners would appreciate not having to pay to listen to her music. Ella also made the decision to keep photos and videos of herself off of the Internet, and insisted that Universal Music Group not promote *The Love Club EP*. Instead, she wanted to let the music's popularity grow on its own, like other artists she admired, such as Burial—an electronic recording artist from London, England—had done. Within hours of the EP's release, Ella had 300 fans!

Lorde performs at Lollapalooza

No Name!

Ella wanted to remain anonymous when she released *The Love Club EP* because she feels "mystery is more interesting."

Love Grows

Ella watched the popularity of *The Love Club EP* grow on the Internet. Canadian singer and songwriter Grimes, who is one of Lorde's musical idols, helped to create a buzz when she tweeted a link to Lorde's SoundCloud page. Soon, the project had more than 60,000 downloads! It was then that Universal Music Group decided to release the EP for sale. After being released on March 8, 2013, *The Love Club EP* shot to fame! It peaked at number two on the record charts in New Zealand and Australia.

Electronica and pop artist Grimes began to record and perform her music while attending university in Montreal, Quebec.

She Said It

"It's weird, because, when you're in the early stages of a project, it's so pure – you're like, 'This will never be tainted.' Then you get further on and you're like, 'I want people to hear this record, so I've got to do something to support it.' I put my music out with no kind of commercial expectation, and found out I was a pop star."

– Interview in *Rolling Stone*, October 28, 2013

Royals

In the summer of 2013, "Royals" was released as a single from *The Love Club EP*. The song topped the charts in New Zealand, Canada, Ireland, and the United Kingdom, and was played on radio stations around the world. In the United States, "Royals" reached number one on the *Billboard* Hot 100 for nine consecutive weeks. That made Lorde the youngest artist, at age 16, to top the charts in more than 25 years.

The baseball uniform of Kansas City Royals legend George Brett inspired Lorde to write her song "Royals."

Lorde wrote "Royals" in just half an hour after seeing an old photo of Kansas City Royals star player George Brett in his baseball uniform. The team's name "Royals" was printed across his shirt. At the time she wrote the song, Lorde had been listening to many rap artists, including Nicki Minaj and Drake, as well as pop singer Lana Del Ray. They all sing about luxurious lifestyles. "Royals" criticizes **materialism** as an unrealistic goal for most people—but there's still a hint of envy there.

Royal Watchers

When they made the music video for "Royals," many of Lorde's schoolmates from New Zealand were in it. Lorde herself is rarely seen in the video. It won the award for best video at the 2013 New Zealand Music Awards.

Pure Heroine

After the release of *The Love Club EP*, Lorde and Joel continued to write songs for her debut album. Before it's release on September 27, 2013, Universal Music Group intentionally leaked lyrics to promote the album. Lorde's lyrics popped up all over New Zealand—on store windows, on the roofs of buses, on street posters outside the Auckland Art Gallery, and were even hidden within classified ads in newspapers. The album, *Pure Heroine*, made a big impression on the music world. Music critics praised the songwriting, as well as Lorde's voice, and the album topped the charts in countries all over the world. Besides "Royals," the album featured "Team," "Tennis Court," and "Glory and Gore."

In June 2014, Lorde released a makeup line with MAC Cosmetics, consisting of black eyeliner and a deep-plum lipstick shade called Pure Heroine.

"Tennis Court" and "Team"

Lorde's second single, "Tennis Court," was released in June 2013. The song describes Lorde's newfound fame, her hometown of Devonport, Auckland, and the friends she grew up with. It also strikes another blow against extravagant lifestyles. The single's music video was filmed in just one shot. Her third single, "Team," was released on September 13, 2013.

At the 29th Annual Rock and Roll Hall of Fame Induction Ceremony, Lorde got to hang out backstage with musicians Kim Gordon, Joan Jett, and St. Vincent (also known as Annie Clark).

Well Read

Lorde credits her mother's writing with having the greatest influence on her own songwriting. But she has said her writing is also inspired by the short story form. Like songs, there is limited space in short stories, so you have to convey meaning in as few words as possible. Some of her favorite short story authors are Raymond Carver, Kurt Vonnegut, Miranda July, and Claire Vaye Watkins.

Touring

When performing for an audience, Lorde doesn't try to create a stage **persona**. Although she confesses to being nervous before performing, her stage presence seems to come naturally to her. She moves across the stage, feeling the music and moving in a twitchy kind of dance. Already, she has headlined many festivals including Lollapalooza in Chile, Brazil, and Argentina. In early 2014, she embarked on a tour to promote *The Love Club EP* and *Pure Heroine*. The tour began in North America, moved to Australia in July, then back to North America the following month.

On tour, Lorde is backed up by only a keyboardist, a drummer, and a sound technician.

Lorde meets Win Butler from Arcade Fire, one of her favorite bands.

Musical Influences

Lorde's influences include artists whose vocals she considers to be interesting. These include electronic artists such as James Blake, and the **experimental rock** bands Yeasayer and Animal Collective. She also admires bands that create stories or big feelings through their lyrics, such as Arcade Fire, Lana Del Rey, and rap artists Kanye West and J. Cole.

Muppet Puppet

The Muppets Studio created a puppet of Lorde, which was auctioned off to raise money for the Starship Children's Hospital, New Zealand's largest pediatric hospital. The Lorde puppet raised more than $3000!

At the 2014 Grammy Awards, Lorde received four nominations. She won twice for "Royals" as Best Pop Solo Performance and Song of the Year.

She Said It

"The kind of clothes that I've found I like to wear over the past year and six months have all been things that make me feel powerful and strong. I wear a lot of pants. I wear a lot of long, structured dresses."
– Interview in *Vogue* magazine, February 20, 2014

The Hunger Games

Lorde recorded a cover of the song "Everybody Wants to Rule the World" by Tears for Fears for the *The Hunger Games: Catching Fire* soundtrack. In the summer of 2014, Lorde announced that she was recording songs for the soundtrack of *The Hunger Games: Mockingjay Part 1*. "Yellow Flicker Beat" was released from the soundtrack in the fall of 2014. The lyrics are based on the movie's heroine, Katniss Everdeen, and the song's mood is as dark and dramatic as the basis of the movie.

The video for "Yellow Flicker Beat" tries to capture the feeling of alienation felt by *The Hunger Games'* Katniss Everdeen.

Two lucky fans won passes to watch Lorde onstage at Coachella. The money from the raffle was donated to charity.

Charity Work

Young as she is, Lorde understands how to use the power of her celebrity to do good in the world. After typhoon Haiyan wreaked havoc in the Philippines in 2013, music artists around the world came together to put forward a record compilation called *Songs for the Philippines*. The album consists of 39 hit singles, including Lorde's song "The Love Club." Proceeds from the album went to those affected by the typhoon. In 2014, through Charitybuzz, she gave two lucky fans passes to sit at the side of the stage during her performance at the Coachella Music and Arts Festival. The proceeds from fan bids supported the Sweet Relief Musicians Fund, which provides financial assistance to struggling musicians.

Strength of Her Convictions

It's not surprising that the subjects of Lorde's songs are about expressing your opinions and being taken seriously. In her personal life, Lorde feels very strongly about the rights of not just teenagers, but of all individuals around the world. Although she was not yet old enough to vote at the time, she recorded a public video in 2014 to encourage young people in New Zealand to act on their right to vote in the national election.

Lorde also refers to herself as a feminist, and is dismayed by the **provocative** portrayal of women and girls in magazines and music videos. She is also concerned about the effect that altering photographs to make women's appearances seem perfect has on the self-esteem of young girls. Her own experience at photoshoots has been that she is asked to pose in a sexy way—even though she is a teenager—or to look beautiful and "confused."

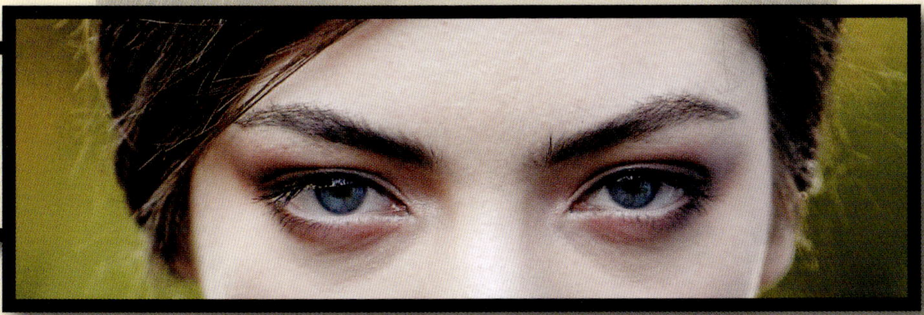

She Said It

"I think I'm speaking for a bunch of girls when I say that the idea that feminism is completely natural and shouldn't even be something that people find mildly surprising. It's just a part of being a girl…And [it's] not something that a hundred different people can define in exactly the same way."
—Interview in *Rookie Magazine*, January 2, 2014

That Kind of Lux

Lorde has found that achieving stardom has its perks. She had never been on an airplane until promoting *Pure Heroine*, and has since traveled to countries all over the world. Her newfound celebrity has given Lorde her own money, and she frequently meets other celebrities, some of whom she has even become good friends with. But her life has not changed that drastically. She and her friends go to the same places they have always gone, except now she is recognized as Lorde, and the paparazzi take pictures of her.

Let's Dance

Lorde got to meet one c her idols, David Bowie. He told her that listenin to her music was like listening to tomorrow.

Friends Lorde and Taylor Swift pose for a selfie, toasting Lorde's 18th birthday with orange juice.

Lorde respects her fans, and takes the time to chat with them and pose for pictures when she can.

She Said It

"I think people don't realize how weird it is to go from being a teenager or being just a human being who has opinions and freely discusses them with other people, to having everything you say scrutinized and taken out of context...That stuff was so weird. But now I've kind of got a handle on it."

– Interview in *Rookie Magazine*, January 2, 2014

More to Come

Fans are waiting for Lorde's second album to be released. With only her debut album under her belt, Lorde still has a lot to express musically. Who knows where this amazing teenager's creativity will take her next!

She Said It

"(If) I wrote my next record about the same stuff I wrote my first record about, I think people listening would be able to tell that I didn't believe it. I'm in a weird position, because obviously I am experiencing being able to buy things that I couldn't afford before…So I'm in an interesting place creatively. But I think people would appreciate me writing honestly…"
– Interview in *Rookie Magazine*, January 2, 2014

Timeline

1996: Ella Marija Lani Yelich-O'Connor is born on November 7, in Takapuna, New Zealand
2001: Lorde begins taking drama lessons
2009: Lorde and her friend Louis McDonald win their school's talent show
2010: Lorde is signed to Universal Music Group
2011: Lorde is paired with Joel Little to make music
2012: *The Love Club EP* is released on SoundCloud in November
2013: Lorde's label commercially launches *The Love Club EP* on March 8
2013: The video for "Royals" wins the award for best video at the New Zealand Music Awards
2013: Lorde's debut album *Pure Heroine* is released on September 27
2013: *TIME* magazine lists Lorde as one of the most influential teens in the world
2013: "Royals" wins the Silver Scroll for outstanding songwriting in original New Zealand pop music
2013: In December, Lorde is nominated for four Grammy awards: Record of the Year, Song of the Year, Best Pop Solo Performance, and Best Pop Vocal Album.
2014: *Pure Heroine* wins two Grammy awards for Best Pop Solo Performance and Song of the Year
2014: Lorde's concert tour begins to promote *The Love Club EP* and *Pure Heroine*
2014: Lorde launches a makeup line with MAC Cosmetics in June
2014: Lorde releases "Yellow Flicker Beat" from *The Hunger Games: Mockingjay Part 1* soundtrack

Glossary

aristocracy A class of people considered to be superior in education, ability, social status, or wealth

artists and repertoire (A&R) manager The person at a record label responsible for finding talent and overseeing the artistic development of the artists

civil engineer A person who plans, designs, and constructs public works such as canals, bridges, roads, and dams

experimental rock Music that uses basic elements of rock, but features unusual compositions and performances

extended play (EP) A musical recording that is too short to be considered a full studio album, and that contains more music than a single

glorify Treating something or someone as greater than would be normally considered

indietronica A type of music that combines pop, indie, and electronica, and consists of music created by synthesizers, electronic keyboards, and drum machines

materialism Putting importance on material objects and comforts

persona The perceived personality of a well-known person, such as a celebrity

producer An individual within the music industry who is responsible for managing the recording of an artist's music

promote To help sell or popularize

provocative Something that suggests impropriety

soul A form of gospel music that was developed in the 1950s

Find Out More

Books

Schwartz, Heather E., *Lorde: Songstress with Style.* (*Pop Culture Bios)* Lerner Publishing Group, 2015.

Shapiro, Marc, *Lorde: Your Heroine.* Riverdale Avenue Books, 2014.

Websites

Lorde
www.lorde.co.nz
Lorde's official site

MTV
www.mtv.com/artists/lorde/
This site features all things Lorde—interviews, videos, photos, and a biography.

Index

About the Author
Adrianna Morganelli holds degrees in English Language and Literature and Fine Arts and has a diploma in Professional Writing. Her professional career includes working as an editor and authoring many non-fiction books for children as well as a children's fiction chapter book.